MONSTERS!

WEREWOLVES

BY PETER CASTELLANO

HOT TOPICS

Gareth Stevens
PUBLISHING

Please visit our website, www.garethstevens.com. For a free color catalog of all our high-quality books, call toll free 1-800-542-2595 or fax 1-877-542-2596.

Library of Congress Cataloging-in-Publication Data

Castellano, Peter.
 Werewolves / Peter Castellano.
    pages cm. — (Monsters!)
 Includes index.
 ISBN 978-1-4824-4098-0 (pbk.)
 ISBN 978-1-4824-4099-7 (6 pack)
 ISBN 978-1-4824-4100-0 (library binding)
 1. Werewolves—Juvenile literature. I. Title.
 GR830.W4C37 2016
 398.24'54—dc23

                              2015032504

First Edition

Published in 2016 by
Gareth Stevens Publishing
111 East 14th Street, Suite 349
New York, NY 10003

Copyright © 2016 Gareth Stevens Publishing

Designer: Samantha DeMartin
Editor: Kristen Nelson

Photo credits: Cover, p. 1 (background) anneleven/Vetta/Getty Images; cover, p. 1 (werewolf) TsuneoMP/Shutterstock.com; text frame Dmitry Natashin/Shutterstock.com; caption box Azuzl/Shutterstock.com; background iulias/Shutterstock.com; p. 5 Francesco Reginato/ The Image Bank/Getty Images; p. 7 Print Collector/Hulton Archive/Getty Images; p. 9 Picture by Tambako the Jaguar/Moment/Getty Images; p. 11 Lupa/Shutterstock.com; p. 13 Time & Life Pictures/The LIFE Picture Collection/Getty Images; p. 15 Barcroft/ Barcroft Media/Getty Images; p. 17 CSA Images/Mod Art Collection/Getty Images; p. 19 Mi.Ti./Shutterstock.com; p. 21 breakermaximus/Shutterstock.com; p. 23 Bob Orsillo/ Shutterstock.com; p. 25 Silver Screen Collection/Moviepix/Getty Images; p. 27 Ernesto Ruscio/Getty Images Entertainment/Getty Images; p. 29 (inset) Bildagentur Zoonar GmbH/ Shutterstock.com; p. 29 (main) Joshua Hultquist/Photolibrary/Getty Images; p. 30 (paw print) Kletr/Shutterstock.com; p. 30 (wolf skin) Kachalkina Veronika/ Shutterstock.com; p. 30 (moon) Razumovskaya Marina Nikolaevna/Shutterstock.com.

Printed in the United States of America

CPSIA compliance information: Batch #CW16GS: For further information contact Gareth Stevens, New York, New York at 1-800-542-2595.

CONTENTS

AT THE FULL MOON

Being outside the night of a full moon can be creepy. If there are no clouds, the moon can be bright, creating shadows everywhere. On a night like this, you might keep an eye out for werewolves!

BEYOND THE MYTH

Throughout history, **myths** about werewolves haven't agreed. There are many stories about when and how one becomes a werewolf.

5

OLD MYTH

Some of the world's oldest myths include men changing into wolves. It's often a **punishment** from the gods. In *The Epic of Gilgamesh*, the goddess Ishtar angrily turns a shepherd into a wolf so he's the enemy of his animals.

BEYOND THE MYTH

Becoming a werewolf can be called lycanthropy. The man turned into a wolf in Ovid's *Metamorphoses* is called Lycaon. Both are based on an old word, *lykos*, that means wolf.

FEAR IN EUROPE

Werewolves are more than men turned into wolves. In most European myths about them, werewolves are wolves at night and men during the day. To those living in **medieval** Europe, werewolves were real and to be feared.

BEYOND THE MYTH

Wolves were a fearsome predator in Europe.
Many fairy tales and stories show them as evil,
including *Little Red Riding Hood*.

9

Stories about werewolves scared so many people, they were hunted during the 16th century. Some stories said werewolves turned their skin inside out to hide their fur during the day. One way to check if someone was a werewolf was by taking their skin off!

BEYOND THE MYTH

In Germany, it was believed that a man could become a werewolf by wearing a belt made of wolf skin. Some of these myths consider becoming a wolf a gift, not a punishment.

11

BEAST OF GÉVAUDAN

From 1764 to 1767, many people were being killed in the French countryside. A huge animal was blamed, and people started to panic. Wolves were killed because people living around the area believed the animal was a werewolf!

BEYOND THE MYTH

According to one source, about 30,000 werewolves were found and killed in France from 1520 to 1630, a time period called the Inquisition.

BELIEF!

Werewolves aren't real. So what made people believe they were? The effects of some **diseases** seem like clues that someone is a werewolf. People with hypertrichosis, for example, grow lots of hair all over their body.

BEYOND THE MYTH

Hypertrichosis is sometimes
called the werewolf disease.

15

People often believed in werewolves in places where wolves lived and many people were being killed. They likely didn't want to think a person was behind the deaths. Instead, the werewolf myth could explain the events.

BEYOND THE MYTH

Sometimes wolves **breed** with other animals. The half-wolves may have been mistaken for werewolves.

THE MODERN WEREWOLF

Werewolves in stories today often have superstrength and supersenses when they're in wolf form. Sometimes, they're said to have bushy eyebrows, curved fingernails, and a strange walk when in human form. Then people can spot them!

BEYOND THE MYTH

In some stories, when a werewolf dies, it becomes a vampire, or a mythical creature that drinks blood. In others, werewolves and vampires are enemies.

In wolf form, werewolves have been shown to look like people with fur and sharp teeth. They might also talk and have very human eyes. Other times, they're huge wolves with hardly a hint of humanity left.

BEYOND THE MYTH

Werewolves aren't unbeatable. Stories say wounds suffered as a wolf carry over into their human form.

TRANSFORMATIONS

Werewolves have often been said to transform, or change, during a full moon. But not every story agrees! Werewolves may have no way to stop their change at the full moon. Or they may be able to choose when they change.

BEYOND THE MYTH

The change from man to wolf is often shown to
be painful as bones grow longer and long, sharp
teeth appear in the mouth.

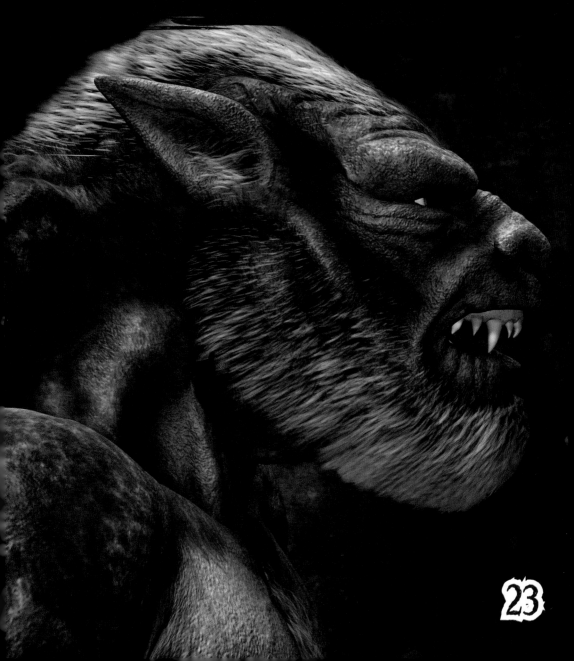

BOOKS, MOVIES, AND TV

Remus Lupin in *Harry Potter and the Prisoner of Azkaban* is a werewolf—but he's able to keep from changing by drinking a **potion**! In the wizarding world, werewolves are looked down on, and he tries to hide it.

BEYOND THE MYTH

The Wolf Man and *Werewolf of London* were some of the early movies that shaped how werewolves are shown today.

In 2011, the show *Teen Wolf* started showing on MTV. It's loosely based on a 1985 movie called *Teen Wolf* starring Michael J. Fox. What would you do if you became a werewolf?

BEYOND THE MYTH

Jacob, a werewolf in the *Twilight* books and movies, is part of a family of werewolves! Taylor Lautner plays Jacob in the movies.

TAYLOR LAUTNER

27

THE SILVER BULLET

If you want to keep a werewolf away, myths say to build a house under a mountain ash tree or get some wolfsbane. Today, stories say the best way to kill a werewolf is with a silver bullet!

WOLFSBANE

BEYOND THE MYTH

In places where wolves don't live, there are similar stories about other animals, such as weretigers in India!

Do You Want to Be a Werewolf?

drink rainwater from a wolf's PAW PRINT

perform the right MAGIC

wear a belt of WOLF SKIN and nothing else

be the child of a WEREWOLF

let the MOON shine on your face on a certain night

FOR MORE INFORMATION

BOOKS

Ferrell, David L. *Shape-Shifters!* New York, NY: PowerKids Press, 2014.

O'Hearn, Michael. *Vampires vs. Werewolves: Battle of the Bloodthirsty Beasts.* Mankato, MN: Capstone Press, 2012.

West, David. *Ten of the Best Monster Stories.* New York, NY: Crabtree Publishing Company, 2015.

WEBSITES

The Legend of Werewolves

kidzworld.com/article/24871-the-legend-of-werewolves

Want to learn more about werewolves in myth and in pop culture? Head here!

Myths, Legends and Stories

wolfcountry.net/stories

Find links to many myths, fables, and more about wolves and werewolves.

breed: to come together to produce babies

disease: illness

medieval: having to do with the Middle Ages, a time in European history from about 500 to 1500

myth: a legend or story

potion: a drink meant to have a magical effect on someone

punishment: something to make someone suffer for a wrong they've done